Narcissistic Abuse

Recovering from a toxic relationship and becoming the Narcissist's nightmare. Healing from emotional abuse and averting the narcissistic personality disorder to get your power back!

Dr. Theresa J. Covert

The follow eBook is reproduced below with the goal of providing information that is as accurate and reliable as possible· Regardless, purchasing this eBook can be seen as consent to the fact that both the publisher and the author of this book are in no way experts on the topics discussed within and that any recommendations or suggestions that are made herein are for entertainment purposes only· Professionals should be consulted as needed prior to undertaking any of the action endorsed herein·

This declaration is deemed fair and valid by both the American Bar Association and the Committee of Publishers Association and is legally binding throughout the United States·

Furthermore, the transmission, duplication or reproduction of any of the following work including specific information will be considered an illegal act irrespective of if it is done electronically or in print· This extends to creating a secondary or tertiary copy of the work or a recorded copy and is only allowed with express written consent from the Publisher· All additional right reserved·

The information in the following pages is broadly considered to be a truthful and accurate account of facts and as such any inattention, use or misuse of the information in question by the reader will render any resulting actions solely under their purview. There are no scenarios in which the publisher or the original author of this work can be in any fashion deemed liable for any hardship or damages that may befall them after undertaking information described herein.

Additionally, the information in the following pages is intended only for informational purposes and should thus be thought of as universal. As befitting its nature, it is presented without assurance regarding its prolonged validity or interim quality. Trademarks that are mentioned are done without written consent and can in no way be considered an endorsement from the trademark holder.

Table of Contents

Introduction

Congratulations on downloading *Narcissistic Abuse* and thank you for doing so.

The following chapters will discuss several topics related to identifying a narcissist, the signs of narcissistic abuse, the short and long-term effects of narcissistic abuse, as well as some tips for dealing with a narcissist and healing after abuse. There is really no way to describe how it feels to have dealt with a true narcissist; only those who have been affected and understand the depths of the abuse of a narcissistic will truly understand what it feels like. It is my hope that, through reading this book, that those who believe they've suffered at the hands of a narcissist or suspect the presence of a narcissistic abuser in their lives will be able to educate themselves so that they can identify and evade the chaos that awaits them.

In chapter 1, we will discuss the basics of narcissism and how the psychological community categorizes different manifestations of a narcissistic personality. We will then cover several different strategies and character traits which are trademark signs of a narcissistic abuser, including gaslighting and choosing targets. We will discuss what it is like to be in a romantic relationship with a narcissistic abuser and the effects of such abuse over time. Finally, we will look at some ways a person can protect themselves from potential narcissistic abuse as well as identify when they might be suffering from abuse and how to get help. The path to recovery from narcissistic abuse can be long and circuitous. The emotional and psychological effects often last for the rest of the person's life, but we must also remember that the human mind has an incredible capacity for healing and rebuilding.

There are plenty of books on this subject on the market, thanks again for choosing this one! Every effort was made to ensure it is full of as much useful information as possible, please enjoy!

Chapter 1: Understanding the Narcissist

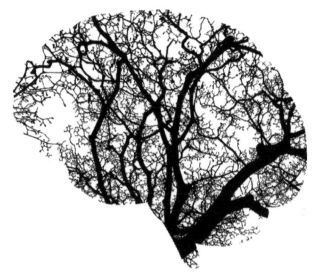

In order to discuss narcissistic abuse, we must first learn about the basic characteristics of a narcissist and how they manifest in their relationships with other people.

Many people will be surprised to learn that there are actually several different subtypes and manifestations of narcissism. For example, a narcissistic personality can be cerebral or somatic. The cerebral narcissist is the individual who believes they are intellectually much more capable and smarter than everyone else. They look down on others and assume as part of their nature that everything they have to offer intellectually is going to be much better than the others' contributions, whether it's

7

an idea or plan of action at work or how best to do a job at home or in school.

The cerebral narcissist is all about impressing others with their mental prowess and may often exaggerate or even make up stories from their lives in order to inflate this reaction from other people. The underlining component to the narcissist's behavior, after all, is self-worship. They worship themselves, but they are also very needy when it comes to receiving praise from others as well. They will put others down if it makes them look better in everyone else's eyes without hesitation.

Then you have the somatic narcissist, who is basically just madly in love with their aesthetic qualities. They are generally very meticulous about their appearances and will do anything to maintain their looks. They are in love with their own reflections and see no faults when they look in the mirror. Think of the guy at the gym who seems to live there, constantly looking at his reflection and showing off for everyone around him. Whenever he sees someone else who looks good, he may go out of his way to demonstrate his superiority in some way. Now, this isn't enough to go on to concretely label someone a narcissist, but it would definitely be familiar territory in terms of how a somatic narcissist might spend his time.

When we talk about narcissism, I will most often refer to the narcissist as a "he." That's because it turns out, there are many more male narcissists than there are female. Psychologists have lots of theories and beliefs about why this is, and we can dig into that a bit deeper later, but know that in general, a narcissist is much more likely to be a man than a woman.

Okay, so we have these two overarching categories of narcissism. Now, let's talk a bit about the four different subtypes of narcissist personalities. These subtypes may be discussed using slightly different terminology in different mediums, but they are broadly uniform when we talk about the different types.

The first subtype is called overt narcissism. Overt narcissism describes a person who is narcissistic and openly displays this personality type. The overt narcissist is who most people think of first when anyone mentions the term narcissism. He is quite loud and boisterous about his personal accomplishments. She will use weapons like shaming and making fun of others in order to make herself look better than everyone else, especially when she feels like her status is being threatened· The overt narcissist does not hesitate to openly take action against others or to bolster their own egos without any regard to how it affects others· This is because one of the basic tenets of narcissism is a general lack of empathy for others· In their minds, there is no one more important than themselves, therefore, whatever they need to do to help themselves is perfectly fine, even if it means stomping all over others· This is often one of the first ways people recognize a narcissist; there is a blatant disregard for others that crosses over into inappropriate and hurtful territory, and they don't even try to hide it because there is zero feelings of shame or empathy· The overt narcissist will feed off of other people's positive reaction to their behavior, making them feel even more entitled to treat others how they want· They are the classic bully and may attract others as a kind of entourage simply because of the confidence and power they exude·

The second subtype of the narcissistic personality is called covert narcissism· This is an interesting one and probably quite controversial, depending on whom we're talking about. The covert narcissist is someone who hides their intentions and motivations behind a curtain of goodwill and humanitarianism. They contribute to charities, volunteer, help friends in need, but they do so with as much spotlight on them as they can conjure. They want to be seen being "good people" because this feeds their self-image of basically being a saint who can do no wrong. They relish the praise they receive from others, people telling them they are so nice and kind and generous when all they really care about is making themselves look good.

The third subtype and one of the most damaging to Thomas victims is the seductive narcissist. This applies to both romantic relationships and nonromantic relationships and refers to the emotional manipulation that takes place in order to tie a person to the narcissist individual through a toxic emotional addiction that is first cultivated through a showering of affection over time, and then suddenly withdrawn. The seductive narcissist is skilled at making his victim feel like they are the most important person in the world to him. He may give gifts and spend lots of money on dates and talk openly about his emotions, feign vulnerability and sincerity, then, once the victim feels attached, will suddenly withdraw, pulling his victim along behind him· This is an especially cruel situation because the victim is being used completely for the sole purpose of the narcissist's pleasure and self-worship· He may not have feelings at all for his victim, but simply enjoys having someone tethered to him under false pretenses· It is a sickening and deeply hurtful experience for the victim once they figure out what is going on if they ever do·

The final subtype is also one of the more damaging types and is the vindictive narcissist· Similar to the overt narcissist, the vindictive narcissist will be quite open with their narcissistic personality traits, but in addition, the vindictive narcissist is set on destroying and tearing down others· This is how they feed their need to rise above everyone else· Their victims could be family members, romantic partners, coworkers, or anyone else they come to view as "in their way" somehow· Their methods for tearing down and destroying other people include all types of emotional and psychological manipulation; whatever works best· They may plant insidious rumors about others in an effort to get people to hate one another or talk about people behind their backs in order to manipulate others' opinions of them. They are the playground bullies who love seeing those they deem weak cry and beg and get emotional. This makes them feel superior and justified in what they do.

In the next chapter, we will discuss how the narcissist interacts and affects those of us in the world we call "empaths." This is perhaps one of the most hurtful and toxic interactions that can happen in the world of narcissism because you are dealing with one individual who cares deeply and feels deeply in connection with others and one individual who is completely void of those feelings. When the narcissist gets his claws into an empath, the results can be devastating.

Chapter 2: The Toxic Attraction between an Empath and a Narcissist

An empath is someone who feels not only their own emotions deeply, but the emotions of others. They are the people at work or at school that react instantly and intensely to both good and bad news shared by their friends and family. Some empaths use their empathic feelings to help others in their professional lives as therapists or in another medical field. Others, perhaps, feel a bit as though they are weighed down by their empathic feelings as they try to manage their own lives while shouldering others' emotions around them. We've all met someone who falls into the empathic category. It is one of the most wonderful experiences a person can have when he/she crosses paths with an empath and is able to form a friendship. This is because you always have someone you can talk to who is really going to understand and feel what you are going through, even if they haven't experienced the exact same circumstances. They understand and feel when you are sad, when you are happy, and everything in between. They are great fun to celebrate with because happiness is infectious and easily radiates into the empath.

There is a danger, though, especially when an empath is also prone to trusting her emotions more than her intellect or gut feelings. Empaths can be too trusting, especially if they are sucked in by someone who seems like they need support. This is where the toxic attraction between an empath and a narcissist can have dire consequences.

Let's demonstrate by painting a scenario. A young adult female is a demonstrable empath and is surrounded by a large group of friends as well as loving family members. She has never been purposefully hurt or manipulated because people love to be around her and value her as a friend. She's helped many of her friends through tough times in their lives through being there and providing a shoulder to cry on. She feels her friends' pain and is willing to go through it alongside them to help them through. When she sees someone in need, she feels very strongly for them and tries to help in any way she can. She is the girl you see going out of her way on the sidewalk to throw some change into the homeless man's bucket or help an elderly woman across the street or an elderly man with is groceries as he struggles to get them into his car. It is very difficult for her to simply ignore or do nothing when she feels someone else's pain or discomfort. Similarly, she is very sensitive to other people's feelings and expressions of anger and frustration. She avoids confrontation at all costs because the feelings are overwhelming for her. She often breaks down after a heated argument as she absorbs the feelings of anger given off by the other person.

Now, a narcissist happens to cross paths with this very kind, empathic person. It might be in a restaurant or at a bar when she is around her friends. He listens to bits and pieces of her conversations with others around her and picks up on the fact that she cares very deeply for the people around her, sharing in their pain and trying to help in any way she can. Perhaps, she sees her consoling a friend in a coffee shop while she almost seems more upset than the friend who actually went through the breakup, or some other situation. The narcissist ticks off items in a checklist which details his perfect victim. We can almost imagine him mentally checking off the boxes with a pen in his mind: naïve, gullible, kind, empathic, and trusting.

In this situation, different types of narcissists may adopt different strategies for making initial contact, and we will talk more about the process of how a narcissist chooses his targets in a later chapter, but for now, let's assume a narcissist decides to lure in this empath by subtly approaching and expressing some kind of sadness. He may hold his head in his hands, breath heavily, let out an exasperated sigh, any number of things to try and get this woman's attention. He may strike up a conversation and gradually work in that he is going through a tough time, gently suggesting that he wants to talk about his problems with her.

At this point, the narcissist is going to look for signals from the young woman. Is she comfortable around him?

Does she feel intimidated? Scared? Is she still unsure and needs some more encouragement? Perhaps he picks up on some signals that she might be attracted to him. This is like getting a golden ticket for the narcissist and serves as his green light to work his way in further.

The narcissist, in this situation, is not going to be intimidated by her having friends around, either. One of the narcissist's overabundant character traits is overwhelming confidence in himself and his attraction. He's going to be able to tell when he's successfully intrigued this woman because it is all he cares about and looks for in other people. He is constantly trying out new strategies and gauging other people's reactions to his talk and behavior. At this point, even if her friends try to tug her away and bring the interaction to an end, the narcissist is going to sit tight and wait for the woman to come to *him.* He's already done his job.

Perhaps the woman, let's call her Claire, comes back a few minutes later to ask if he is ok or if he needs to talk more. The skilled narcissist might speak reassuringly to her while looking at her with eyes that suggest he appreciate having her around. He may make a subtle gesture, like touching her hand or arm, in order to gauge her new comfort level with him. He knows how to pretend like he needs support but does not want to interfere with Claire's fun night, which she will find endearing. The night will either end with Claire abandoning her friends in favor of helping out this attractive man who is clearly in pain and in need of support, or she will give him her number so that they may talk later. Either way, the narcissist can consider the play a win.

What is so dangerous in this situation is that the narcissist truly will feel absolutely no remorse for the emotional roller coaster he is about to put Claire through. He is going to revel in her attention and his ability to manipulate her emotions and actions toward whatever end he desires. He's going to know when he's managed to form an attachment that she feels is a real connection and when to pull back so that she craves being with him. He will work his way into her mind and perhaps even cause her to question her reality.

In the next chapter, we will discuss gaslighting—what it is and how it may be used by the narcissist. It is another effective tool which many narcissists learn to master because it offers so much in terms of being able to control another person's thought patterns and behaviors. You may have heard the term in relation to another form of mental manipulation called brainwashing. These terms refer to very real and very hurtful forms of manipulation that can lead to long-term confusion and emotional distress. We'll look at an example using the narcissist and our empath, Claire.

Chapter 3: The Gaslighting Narcissist

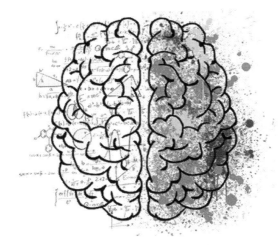

One of the things which make narcissism both fascinating and terrifying is that it can be difficult to work out exactly what makes them tick and what their specific motivations and objectives are. We know broadly that one of the main motivations for a narcissist in his life is to garner recognition and praise from others, but what about on a small scale, with an individual victim? Sometimes, it seems almost as though the narcissist is destroying a person's emotional health just for fun or to see how far he can go. It is a sick and depressing thing to think about. But what else could be motivating a person to treat another human being this way?

Perhaps, we can get a little bit closer by looking at some more of the fundamental characteristics of a narcissistic personality. We've already discussed the general lack of empathy, which pretty much applies across the board in terms of the different narcissist subtypes. But there is another important aspect of the narcissist which is the one thing he tries to hide more than anything, and that is insecurity.

It is important to note that people are not born narcissists, the personality is formed as a result of many different factors involving nature and nurture which are too complex and various to nail down on a general scale. However, when we look at a narcissist's history, it is sometimes possible to hypothesize as to what facets of his upbringing/childhood/adolescence may have contributed to his eventual turning into a narcissist. One of the reasons it feels so imperative to figure out why a narcissist is this way is the apparent meaninglessness and lack of reason involved in using emotionally manipulative tactics like gaslighting on another human being.

What exactly is gaslighting and how does it affect a victim over time?

Essentially, gaslighting is a manipulative process that, over time, causes the victim to question various aspects of his/her reality. To get a clearer picture of what I mean, let's look at some of the warning signs that someone is gaslighting you.

The biggest and most obvious telltale sign is when the person tells obvious, blatant lies. They may be able to look you straight in the face and tell a lie that you may or may not be absolutely sure is false. There is a calculated reason for the narcissist's confidence in himself and this tactic, and it has probably worked for him before. He is going to continue to lie to you until you start to question whether or not you actually know what's going on. People who are confident enough to lie like this, like narcissists, are going to be very effective in their delivery. It will be very difficult to counter their claims because they seem so sure about themselves and what they are claiming to be true.

Another warning sign occurs when the narcissists start to deny that they even said something when you know that they did. It's been said that if at any point in your relationship you feel the need to actually record a conversation, you should get your guard up because this is a pretty good sign that you're being gaslighted. The gaslighting narcissist will also use things and people that are precious to you and turn them into emotional weapons against you. They may back up their claims about you and your flaws with reasonable-sounding arguments, perhaps presenting them in a matter-of-fact way, as everyone knows about this except you. When they've managed to convince you that there is something wrong with you, just like they say, then they will continue to wear you down over time using other flaws or convincing you to isolate yourself from other family and/or friends, even your children.

It can be incredibly frustrating for the victim in a gaslighting situation because the perpetrator's words are often not going to line up with the person's actions. He will say things to you perhaps even lift you up and give you encouragement. But then his behavior may contradict what he has said to you, making you feel like his words are meaningless, or perhaps that you are doing something to cause him not to follow through with what he says.

Let's look at the example with Claire. Perhaps, after a few conversations, the narcissist, let's call him Mark, sees that Claire is growing more attracted to him. He has carefully constructed his story and conversation so as to portray exactly who he wants her to see, even though it isn't genuine. Let's say their relationship grows and he is able to convince her that there are some things about herself that she should work on. Maybe he brings up something about her personality that he overheard one of her friends' making a comment on. Mark begins to plant seeds of insecurity, doubt, and confusion based around the things that he knows she values. He may promise her the world, then seem to fall away completely until she comes begging for him to return to her. He then uses this opportunity of vulnerability to tell her that he would be a lot happier with her if she just fixed this or that thing, maybe it's her appearance or her job, or something else. Gaslighting comes into play when he begins to feed her lies and confuse her about the things that he has said which contradict his behavior. Any time she tries to call him out, he responds very confidently and convincingly, letting her know that she is incorrect. The key here is that he is going to make small steps toward this end over time. It is a slow burn, and Claire is going to suddenly find herself buried deep in her confusion before she even realizes what is going on. Things that she used to be so sure of will fall away and meld into the reality Mark wants to design for her.

The trap is insidious and can go on for years or even decades. The skilled narcissist knows that the more they can confuse you, the more control they can exert over you. They work to make you emotionally vulnerable so that you feel you need him to guide you through. Mark may take steps to turn even Claire's closest friends against her, and then blame them for all the emotional turmoil she is going through. At this point, Clair has developed an emotional dependency and feels like she is nothing without Mark.

The final straw, and the mark of success in the narcissist's mind would be to actually convince you that you are crazy, that you have no idea what you're talking about when you try to call him out on his lies or behavior. Once they can shut this down and make you totally question what's really going on around you, then they have complete control over you. They may feel like keeping up the charade and pulling you around further, or they may get bored and decide to move on to a completely new challenge, seeing as they've conquered you.

If and when Claire finally comes to the realization of what's been done to her, she may start to wonder, why her? What did she do to deserve this? For any victim of narcissistic abuse, this is a question that he/she will likely struggle with. After all, depending on how far the abuse has gone, the victim is going to have very low self-esteem and confidence, having been beaten down emotionally to feel worthless and stupid. So what is the answer to the burning question, why me?

Chapter 4: No Random Targets: He Chose You

Make no mistake; the fact that a person is targeted has nothing to do with chance. In other words, the narcissist is not just going up to people randomly or based on one or two outward characteristics. The narcissist is a calculated thinker with a detailed plan in his head that is as natural to him as breathing. When a person is targeted by a narcissist, it is because this person fulfills many requirements which complete the picture of the perfect victim, similar to the checklist Mark was ticking off in his head as he observed Claire at the bar.

There are several characteristics and strengths which narcissists tend to target when they decide to break down another human being. Many people think that narcissists go after people who seem hurt or broken in some way. Well, this is both true and false. It's true that many narcissist abuse victims have some kind of pre-existing insecurity or source of pain in their lives, but this is not necessarily the main reason a narcissist would target them. You may think that because someone is weak, the narcissist is eager to make easy prey of them. But the truth is, most narcissists want to enjoy a challenge. Picking up an injured animal just to poke and prod an already broken-down creature would not be much fun or much of a challenge.

Instead, narcissists actually target those people who possess some aspect of personality or life circumstance that the narcissist doesn't believe they deserve or should have. It doesn't even have to be jealousy; a narcissist simply doesn't like seeing other people besides themselves find success or power. For this reason, the target of a narcissist may possess skills and character traits that define quite successful, strong people. The key is that their targets also ideally have a large amount of demonstrable empathy and compassion. In fact, the stronger and more intelligent the victim, the more satisfaction the narcissist is going to get from breaking them down.

So, let's complete the picture of an ideal narcissist victim. Of course, this isn't going to be a perfect example to fit every narcissist; there are going to be variances. But we know from research that the narcissist tends to target victims with certain sets of strengths and character traits.

Let's use Claire again as our example. We already know that Claire is an empath. She feels others' emotions as well as her own very strongly, and she feels that it is her duty to go out of her way to help others whenever she can. Let's say that she is also known to be someone with a lot of integrity.

Someone with high integrity is likely to be true to their word, hardworking, and honest with others. When they promise that they can make a deadline at work and it turns out to be a little tighter than they'd anticipated, they are going to work extra hard to make sure they follow through, even though they have to skip a meal or skip date night whatever they may have had planned before· This is an attractive trait for the narcissist because if he can successfully get his hooks in this victim, he knows he's going to be able to use feelings of obligation to coerce her into doing things she may not necessarily have done under different circumstances· Perhaps, he will be able to trick Claire into promising something based on an emotional need, then have to cancel other important plans that she's overlooked because she was preoccupied with the narcissist's incessant attention-seeking behaviors·

Claire, as an ideal victim, is also going to betray some source of emotional trauma or weakness which will make itself evident as the narcissist crawls his way into her mind· We can take a few pointers from the experiences of people who have fallen victim to cults·

One of the most effective strategies recruiters have used to get people too sucked into a radical new way of thinking in line with a cult is to find what it is that person is secretly desperate to find satisfaction for· Many people who are very lonely will latch on to a person and what they are saying simply in reaction to their showing the victim a measure of kindness and attention· There are many people out there who are so filled with pain and who feel isolated· When someone gives them an opportunity to find support for their pain, it is very easy for the person to also accept many other tenets and belief systems alongside that comfort·

Perhaps, a person who is down on their luck in the financial department comes upon a recruiter, whom he doesn't yet know is a recruiter, and this person starts a conversation· The recruiter commiserates with this individual, saying she also has some money issues· Then she goes on to say how she found relief through this group of people who work together and live together, relieving themselves of financial burdens connected with housing, transportation, etc· The recruiter makes it sound like heaven on earth, and soon, the man is brought in to the group and introduced to others· The source of the pain of the victim is always going to be addressed before introducing any kind of belief systems because it is imperative to hook the victim through emotional need before you can introduce new thought patterns·

The narcissist is going to employ a similar tactic in many instances, especially if they manage to get the victim to open up early in the interaction. There is nothing more thrilling to the narcissist than getting an otherwise strong, independent, and confident individual to open up about their vulnerabilities. The narcissist will use this information against the victim, playing up those things which tear the victim down emotionally, then building up a feeling of reliance and dependence on the narcissist to relieve these negative feelings.

If, after a few conversations with Claire, Mark has uncovered the fact that she's had a troubling childhood because of an abusive father, then Mark has a new set of shiny ammunition which is always available to tap in to whenever he needs to bring her down a notch or circumvent the defense mechanisms she has in place to deal with those old feelings. Mark will continue to gather and download information as he constantly observes Claire's behavior and mannerisms throughout their interactions.

What's fascinating also is that the narcissist is going to be able to do his dirty work whether or not the victim is alone or with others. That's because he knows how to covertly exercise his strategies while in private so that they resonate even when they are with others whom the victim feels comfortable around. The narcissist may pull away from the victim in order to asses how long it will take for her to come back to him of her own free will, perhaps choosing to be with him instead of over with her group of friends. This effect will grow gradually over time as he continues to cultivate a sense of dependency on his victims. Eventually, the victim will be so attached and confused that her other relationships may fall by the wayside.

So, we have an idea of the narcissist's modus operandi when it comes to one-on-one initial interactions, but how does the narcissist operate in general? What are some of the common mannerisms and behaviors that manifest in public or with family? In the next chapter, we will take a look at some of the ways narcissists behave and interact in various social settings.

Chapter 5: The Narcissist as a Social Creature

As we've established thus far, the narcissist is basically concerned solely with himself and his effect on others. It all seems like a game from the outside as onlookers analyzing the various behaviors and tactics narcissists employ. But for the narcissist, the reality is that she desperately needs the attention to cloak a likely very deep foundation of insecurity. This insecurity may stem from one of a thousand different experiences, but the root of the narcissist's drive tends to be a very deep need for constant admiration and validation, even though they don't value others in terms of intellectual capability. One can imagine the narcissist in the middle of a group at a party sharing knowledge on a given topic. Someone from the group compliments his thought process and the narcissist looks pleased for only a moment before scoffing audibly; he probably doesn't even know what I'm talking about, etc.

So what are some of the common social behaviors displayed by a narcissist? Let's look at several.

The narcissist is often knowledgeable, at least enough to impress himself and those in his immediate social circles. He may be loud and boisterous in an effort to show off his intellect, gaining favor from those around him because he seems like an affable, fun-loving guy. He will know how to work for a crowd and let them feel involved in the conversation only to captivate them with some pearl of wisdom or a carefully thought-through joke. The narcissist will want to maintain the façade of always being surrounded by friends who love being around him. His company may change often as he moves from one group to the next, entering and exiting conversations as he sees fit, always on the prowl for a potential victim who may be able to help him climb in some way. Underneath this façade is the fact that the narcissist is going to have very few if any, true friends. Aside from victims, the narcissist does not see friendship as necessary because he doesn't need anything from anyone. No one can offer him anything more than what he can offer himself over the long term. He refuses to interact with people who are mostly not as intelligent, and if he finds someone as intelligent, then he's going to do everything he can to destroy them or tear them down in some way. This is how he operates naturally. For whatever reason, he moves throughout the world on the constant lookout for ways to bolster himself above others while simultaneously tearing everything else around him down. Anyone who may initially try to cultivate a friendship will probably catch on to his superficiality quite quickly. The narcissist will only be able to fake intimacy for so long and to a certain extent because he truly does not feel anything for any other people.

In the work setting, the narcissist is going to know exactly who he needs to please and gain favor with in order to climb the corporate ladder. A skilled narcissist will know how to employ things like personality mirroring in order to make himself as amenable as possible to the boss or important coworker or supervisor. The narcissist is really going to know how to present himself in order to get themselves close to the people who are going to help them. But there are some triggers which are going instantly encourage a defensive or aggressive response, and these would be things to watch out for if you suspect someone to be a narcissist.

Oftentimes, a narcissist's stories or sharing of knowledge is going to be exaggerated or even made up in an effort to make himself look good. If the accuracy of this knowledge is challenged in any way, it's going to trigger a response of superiority and disdain, as if to say, what do you know about anything? Don't tell me I'm wrong, you have no idea what you're talking about, etc. Even if you confront the narcissist with point blank proof that their story is incorrect, they will defend themselves and insist that everyone else is lying or an idiot, etc. There is no end to the denial that a narcissist may employ to keep from ever admitting fault to any extent in nearly any situation. They never feel as though they owe anyone an explanation for their behavior. They will convey that they either believe you don't deserve to understand or you are too dumb to understand, etc. It is utterly pointless to try and argue a differing point of view with a narcissist because he is not going to respect you or care enough to try seeing things differently from his own point of view.

Within the family, there are all kinds of additional nuances and character traits which may stem from various earlier experiences in the narcissist's childhood. Let's look at an example.

Let's say that Mark was an only child and that he was pretty isolated throughout his childhood. His parents lavished him with gifts and gave him what he wanted in terms of money, but they never really spent much time appreciating who he was as a person or addressing him emotionally. Everything was about physical performance in sports of academic performance in school. He would get to go on expensive trips with groups from school and he would bring home trophies and the family would praise him and hang up his achievements all over the home, etc. But say he was struggling with a bully at school or felt sad about something someone said or felt insecure about some physical feature. His parents may have been dismissive and unwilling to address his emotional issues and let him wallow in his emotional pain without any support whatsoever· This could culminate, over time, in a sense that emotions don't matter, and since no one cared about how he felt, he has no desire to care about anyone else's feelings either· He may carry a sense of resentment toward his parents for the rest of his life, but because of the many praises he received for his academic and physical accomplishments, he also harbors a deep pride and sense of superiority over others· This is a great recipe for a future narcissist·

Oftentimes, the traits of a narcissist are overlooked by family members out of fear or simple denial· We know that it is quite common for parents to overlook the faults of their children, especially if they are a bit egotistical or even narcissistic themselves· If they are never at fault themselves, there is no way they could ever have a faulty child, after all· No, their children are quite perfect!

Overindulging a child in this way is also a good indicator of a future adult who is going to be overly arrogant and dismissive of others· The point at which arrogance crosses over into narcissism varies by person but always stems from foundational experiences, often consistent experiences over a long period of time, like overindulgent or under-indulgent parents. Only children are often subjected to feelings of loneliness, and if they are spoiled by the parents, they may gain a sense of entitlement that carries on into adulthood, coupled with a broken sense of empathy due to that prolonged isolation. Unfortunately, research has shown that in nearly 100% of narcissist cases, the narcissist will never be able to change and somehow learn how to "undo" the damage which led to their narcissism in the first place.

Chapter 6: Narcissism in the Relationship

Now that we have a basic understanding of the characteristics of the narcissist and how he/she interacts socially on a broad scale, let's take a close look at how a relationship unfolds between a narcissist and an unsuspecting victim.

We will go back to our example involving Mark and Claire.

At the beginning of a romantic relationship with a narcissist, part of the scheme is that Mark is going to make Claire feel like she has found a regular Prince Charming. He will be everything for her and shower her with love and affection. He will give her everything she needs emotionally, and everything will seem perfect...for a while. Remember what they say: If it seems too good to be true, it usually is.

This beginning "honeymoon" phase is essentially the hook that is designed to get Claire really craving his constant affection. He will give everything to her that she wants sexually and be everything she needs in every other respect. Mark will be like a drug, and soon she will become addicted, even before realizing it. Even the most upstanding, strong, morally conscious, and intelligent people are still human beings with desires. Skilled narcissists are going to get under your skin and learn your deepest desires in order to get their claws into you. Once this happens, you are at their mercy unless you pick up on the signs and run as fast as you can in the other direction!

But, unfortunately, Claire does not see any of the signs of narcissism because she has never met a narcissist who was trying to manipulate her. She never surrounded herself with people who were anything other than kind and compassionate, just like her. She loves that Mark has shown his vulnerable side, and he lets her feel like she is helping him through his pain, giving her a sense that she is giving as well as she is receiving. But over time, this will slowly fade away and reveal itself to not be the case any longer.

After a couple of months, perhaps, things will start to shift, as they always do. The timing will vary based on how the narcissist's plans are proceeding. But soon, the once overindulgent boyfriend is going to turn into something different, but at this point, Claire is madly in love with Mark, and what's worse, she trusts him. He starts to employ those emotional and psychological games which work to gradually tear down her self-esteem and confidence. He will introduce flaws and problems with her friends and family and incite arguments between Claire and the people in her life she loves and values. This will serve to slowly isolate her from those people she once trusted as she leans more and more on Mark, trusting in what he tells her because he otherwise gives her what she needs...until he doesn't.

The emotional games will gradually tear Claire down until she is just a shadow of her former self. The narcissist may have already employed gaslighting techniques or just now begin to introduce them as she focuses on the things that she now perceives are flaws in her character, her body, or her personality. Every now and then, she will get a glimpse of the Mark she knew when they'd first met, and this will keep her going for another period of time. But it will gradually start to dawn on her that things are not what they seem.

One of the first things victims in his situation might pick up on is the fact that the narcissist will be careless about consistency and repetitiveness because they do not care what others think or feel as a result. Mark will not necessarily value how his behavior in public reflects on Claire and may openly brag and show off and even flirt with other women right in front of her. When she goes to confront him about this behavior, he will easily deny it and tell her she is making things up—another symptom of gaslighting. It depends on the victim how far this will go. Some people are strung along for years and years. Eventually, the narcissist will simply disappear and then reappear sporadically, telling his victim that he is unsure about things and that he feels insecure about their relationship, perhaps pointing out things that the victim has done wrong in the relationship that makes him doubt her commitment, etc. The narcissist will use anything and everything at this point to inflict pain and make the victim feel like they need to make up for something they've done.

Eventually, the game is going to end, one way or another. Mark will have gotten bored with Claire and decided to move on. But oftentimes, the narcissist will not let go for a very long time, even if they are leaving for long periods of time in between their reappearances. Depending on how strong their chains have become connected to their victims, the victims will simply wait and hope and pray until the next time they see their narcissist partners. The emotional pain and control have run so deep that they do not feel they can live any other way.

When we think of women in physically abusive relationships, many people find it too easy to simply pass judgment on the women, suggesting that she just needs to leave, she just needs to leave... The fact is until you've experienced the kind of emotional abuse and manipulation exercised by an abusive partner, it is impossible to understand just how much a person can twist another human being's reality. Abuse victims often cite how they simply slipped into a state of denial or were so convinced that they were the problem in the relationship that they simply tolerated the abuse and blamed themselves for it happening. It is a sad but true reality. Don't ever pass judgment on an abuse victim until you really know what you're talking about. And even then, we must all realize that each one of us is very unique and that we all have different constitutions, strengths, and weaknesses. How many times have you heard it from someone that, they never thought they'd be dumb enough to fall for that, etc.

It's important to not internalize a feeling of being "dumb" if you've fallen victim to narcissistic abuse. The fact is that these people do nothing with their lives except getting better and better at manipulating and hurting others. They are professionals, and they are experts. You are not an idiot for being human and having feelings. You have simply run into someone who knows exactly how to take advantage of your common human decency and kindness.

After the cycle of abuse ends and you've finally gotten free of the narcissist relationship, I hope that you can appreciate that you are lucky to have broken free at all. Many victims are strung along for the rest of their lives only to die in misery and in isolation without ever having received what they really needed and wanted from a romantic partner. What a victim goes through emotionally over the course of a narcissist abuse experience is harrowing and the effects are long-lasting. In the next chapter, we will talk about the emotional upheaval of ending a relationship with a narcissist and the effects of this experience in the long term.

Chapter 7: Effects of Narcissistic Abuse over Time

The effects of experience with narcissistic abuse can be devastating and long-lasting. Comorbid conditions like depression and anxiety are common after going through a period of emotional manipulation and may leave the victim with trust issues and anxieties that last the rest of their lives.

The signs of depression can vary from person to person, but the emotional turmoil caused by narcissistic abuse can trigger depression in people who have never experienced depression before in their lives. As a result of techniques like gaslighting, a person may begin to internalize a completely false reality about themselves, believing themselves to be flawed fundamentally, undeserving of love, and selfish. The narcissist understands that the more he can make a victim feel like they are doing something wrong, the more he can convince them to do things to correct the error or make up for what they've done. This is especially thrilling because the narcissist realizes that the victim has not actually done anything wrong; he's just that good at manipulation. It is really a matter of getting a notch on the belt for someone like the narcissist, and the effects on the victim do not garner any guilt or shame from him.

Depression manifests in a prolonged emotional state of hopelessness or helplessness. Many sufferers hear voices in their heads that constantly tell them they are worthless or stupid or that they are not enough. This voice may manifest as the narcissist's voice himself in a victim of narcissistic abuse. The voice may be persistent for days on end, especially at night when relaxation becomes impossible.

Anxiety is another possible aftereffect of narcissist abuse

and especially common in instances where there is a history of physical abuse as well. The anxiety will often stem from the creation of doubt and destruction of self-esteem that goes along with narcissistic abuse. A once confident person may let down their guard just long enough for the narcissist to poke their head in and plant an idea about how that failed relationship was their fault, or they are really too fat to be wearing that, or that supervisor at work probably doesn't think you're good enough, etc. Whatever a narcissist can sink their teeth into, they will do it.

Towards the end of the abuse cycle, the victim may finally start to see the light and attempt to get as far away from the perpetrator as possible. This may or may not be successful, depending on what else the narcissist has going on at the time. He may have already found someone else to concentrate on, so you may find some peace and quiet, at least until they get bored and come find you again. Other times, the narcissist may completely disappear from your life without a trace and you may never hear from him again. This may initially feel tragic, as you've still got to deal with the emotional attachment that was cultivated. But soon, you will start to realize that you are a survivor of an abuser and you are lucky to be free.

One technique many abuse victims utilize after an experience like this is therapy, either in a group setting or a one-on-one setting. It can be very helpful to talk to others who have been through a similar situation and it is important to be able to ground yourself in the truth that you were not stupid or immoral or bad or not enough; you were manipulated, just like the others in your group. Talking to these individuals may go a long way in finding yourself again after a long and dreadful experience of narcissistic abuse.

There are several typical emotions and cycles of thought that victims of narcissistic abuse experience immediately following the end of the relationship. The victim is usually quite tired and worn out, and this may last weeks or even months. Emotional exertion takes a toll just like muscle exertion. It will take time to recover and heal from this stress. You may feel disgusted with yourself for having fallen victim to something like this. As I've stressed before, it is very important that you try to talk to someone or wrap your mind around the reality that you are not at fault. You are not stupid. Someone who is an expert at emotional manipulation with zero sense of remorse has taken complete advantage of you and your pain.

It is common for the victim to go through feelings of guilt and shame. Let these feelings run their course, but again, it is important to put yourself in an environment which supports the truth that you have survived an ordeal, not committed a horrendous crime.

Panic attacks and anxiety may go hand-in-hand for a while after the abuse. Some people get out without experiencing symptoms like this, but others will need to address the issue through talk therapy and/or drug therapy.

You will feel a big blow to your self-esteem, and this may take some time to build back up again. Try to surround yourself with people who love you and who care for you. You will likely go through all kinds of emotional fallout, and it is good to let it out when you need to. You may feel like crying or screaming or releasing your emotions in some other way. Perhaps, you may find it helpful to join a gym and go punch a punching bag for an hour. Whatever you need to do, try to express and release that emotion rather than bottling it up inside of you. This will only make the eventual release much worse and may even cause toxicity and additional emotional and psychological turmoil.

It will be natural to have a desire to think things through and figure him out. But it is important that you not exert too much effort on this, because the actions of a narcissist are contradictory, unreasonable, and sporadic. Narcissists do whatever they need to do to make themselves feel good at the time. If the next day they need to make a 180 and do something different, they aren't going to care whether or not it makes sense to you; they'll just do it. Don't try to figure them out. They're not worth it. And what's much more important; do not put yourself through the ordeal of thinking you can be an amazing enough influence that you can change them and make them not narcissistic anymore. I promise you, this is a waste of time. And likely they are going to use this as just another opportunity to manipulate you in some way. Believe me, cut your losses and move on. Don't ever look back. You may feel tempted from time to time to try and hunt this person down again. Maybe you want to tell them what they really did to you or try and explain to them what they've done wrong in an effort to gain some kind of affection or hint of the things they once showed you at the beginning of the relationship. It is so important that you realize that it was all an act—a complete façade. You must let these things go and move forward. And don't convince yourself that all men are awful and not worth the trouble. Relationships are always going to present unique difficulties, but I promise you that it is possible to find a partner who is respectful, loving, and who shares interests with you. Don't give up.

In the next chapter, we will discuss some tips for dealing with a narcissist in your life. Perhaps, this individual is a member of your family or someone who is simply not going away any time soon. There are ways you can compromise and deal with their existence in your life.

Chapter 8: Advice for Dealing with a Narcissist and the Aftermath of Abuse

Before we address some advice for dealing with a narcissist and the aftermath of abuse, it is important that we outline some of the key indicators that you are indeed suffering from narcissistic abuse syndrome.

The first and foremost signal to yourself that you are suffering from dealing with a narcissist in a toxic relationship is the persistent feeling that you are alone. If you come home each day and see your boyfriend, eat meals with your boyfriend, sit in front of a TV with your boyfriend, then go to bed next to a boyfriend, but still feel like you've spent the whole day alone, it's because you might be dealing with a narcissist who is only presenting to you a mirage of the relationship you thought you were living. There is an absence of feeling underneath the actions that leave you feeling lost, confused, and very lonely. If you feel this constantly and are unsure of where the feeling came from, this may be a sign of narcissistic abuse syndrome.

If you are constantly struggling with the feeling that you are just not good enough for anyone, especially your boyfriend/partner, then you may be suffering from narcissistic abuse syndrome. Narcissists are very good at tearing down their victims' self-esteem and convincing them through both subtle and not-so-subtle strategies that they are messing things up, constantly making mistakes, etc. They may make fun of you and laugh at you or mock you and make you feel small. This abuse leads you to believe that you are worthless and that you would never be good enough for anything you want to accomplish in life.

You may feel suffocated by the relationship itself as your narcissist partner attempts to hijack your personal life and everything that existed before he/she entered your life. It is a trademark strategy of exercising control to isolate the victim from those he/she once trusted and loved. It is the narcissist's goal to make him/herself the only person you lean on for anything kind of support.

Another sign of narcissistic abuse syndrome is the realization that you've become a different person in terms of belief systems, morals, principles, or other characteristics which were once at the core of who you are. If your partner has managed to change these essential things about you and they don't seem right, it is a sign that you've got some toxic forces at work doing everything they can to make you into a different person that serves the purposes of only the narcissist.

Narcissists often utilize outright name-calling in an effort to belittle and gradually break down a victim's sense of self-worth. This practice may not be overt in the beginning, but instead, be framed as a kind of joke and kidding by the narcissist. He may say while giggling, "You're just overreacting because you're too sensitive." Comments like these may seem innocent at first, but over time with persistent use, these things can be internalized by the victim until the accusations became a reality for them. They may start to believe these things which at first they didn't feel were affecting them in any damaging way.

Finally, the cycle of something called "hurt and rescue" can take such a toll on a victim as to lead to life-long emotional anxieties and struggles. With this technique, the narcissist introduces stress through an event or an argument or an accusation and then gives the victim the silent treatment for a certain amount of time. They may use a tactic other than the silent treatment, but whatever they choose to do, the object is to relieve that stress or silence it for an amount of time. The silent treatment, when used in this way, triggers a fear of abandonment that is innate in pretty much every human being out there. This makes it an inescapable strategy to induce pain, as long as the victim feels attachment and emotion for the perpetrator.

The rescue stage entails the perpetrator coming back and relieving that fear of abandonment, but now, the victim has learned to be afraid whenever the cycle starts again, anticipating that period of staged abandonment, or silence.

Over time, this technique becomes a powerful strategy for control and manipulating behaviors because the feelings associated with abandonment can be so strong and hurtful. Each one of us is hardwired to crave attention, love, and affection, so when someone offers this then abruptly takes it away, we learn to do whatever we need to do to avoid having that attachment leave us again, even if it means apologizing for something we didn't even do, much to the narcissist's delight.

When you feel sure you are dealing with a narcissist in a romantic relationship, you need to seek support in getting out and away as soon as possible. Educate yourself on the tactics used by narcissists to keep that feeling of attachment in you and do everything you can to resist it and break free. Remind yourself again and again that it's all been an act and nothing you were feeling attached to is real.

If you are dealing with a narcissist who is not a romantic partner but still an unavoidable part of your life, your best defense is going to be constant awareness and alertness to any schemes and manipulation the narcissist may be trying to employ on you. It would be unwise to start an all-out war on the narcissist since his whole being is centered on crushing others and he will surely be able to invest more time and emotional energy into hurting you than you will in hurting him. Besides, you're not that kind of person!

Even though you may feel anger, letting your guard down and losing control is exactly what the narcissist wants you to do, so do not give him the satisfaction.

As always, strength in numbers is a good rule of thumb to follow. If you are feeling vulnerable or susceptible to a narcissist in your purview, recruit others to support you and help form a barrier. Let the narcissist know that you are too smart to fall for his schemes and that you are not going to give an inch. Create a thick skin around yourself and prepare for some demeaning insults designed to rile you up. You don't have to give in to these. Form your support group and move on with your life. When the narcissist sees that you've all but become immune to his charms, he will look elsewhere and leave you alone. Be on the lookout for others whom he may be targeting and be sure to let them know what's going on if you think they are also in danger. This will probably trigger a defensive response, but the key is to maintain your composure and remind yourself of your reality and your standing. Don't buy into the narcissist portraying himself as more than what he is. Inside, he is just an insecure little boy trying to validate himself through other people's praises. He does not have power over you or those you love. You are stronger than this person because you know the strength and power of genuine love and affection.

In our final chapter, we will discuss some advice and tips for those who have gone through the abuse from a narcissist and are on the journey towards recovery. We will also discuss how you can arm yourself against future narcissist abuse. As always, I encourage you to educate yourself as much as possible about the narcissist and his various schemes. Knowledge, after all, is power.

Chapter 9: Recovery

I believe strongly in the power of self-healing, and I believe that any degree of emotional pain can be addressed through self-care and healing practices over time· It may be a long road and will certainly not be easy, but with proper support and belief in yourself, it is possible to move past the experience of narcissistic abuse to a large degree· You may not be able to erase the effects entirely, but it is possible to move and live a healthy, productive, and emotionally stable life after even the most damaging of emotional experiences· This is because the human brain has an incredible capacity to rewire itself and relearn how to live and love through healthy habits and new thought cycles that will take the place of the old, destructive thought cycles.

First of all, grab an old journal or buy yourself a nice new one. Many survivors of abuse can attest to the power of simply writing out and processing your feelings through words. There may be many aspects of your experience with narcissistic abuse that you have yet to really address or wrap your mind around. Remember, the key here is not to focus on figuring out or working out the mental manipulations of your abuser. The focus here should be on working through the feelings you experienced and then work to disentangle those negative feelings from the thought cycles feeding them. For example, you may have heard your abuser constantly accusing you of being too fat or too skinny. Write about how this made you feel, then reinforce the fact that there is nothing wrong with your body and that this was just one of many tools your abuser used to break you down. Letting these feelings bring you pain over and over is simply a type of surrender to your abuser. Replace these negative thoughts with positive, affirming thoughts about your beautiful body and what it has done for you. Expressions of gratitude can also go a long way to dispel feelings of worthlessness and emptiness. Again, it won't dispel all of your negative feelings right away. Forming positive habits of thoughts takes time, but it is well worth it. Don't let the incessant negativity from your past relationship dominate your future thoughts.

Another way to help you process and move through negative emotion to release this energy is through physical exercise or contemplative movement therapy, like yoga. There are many yoga practices designed specifically to help you move your thoughts through negative emotions into a more positive space. Cultivating a healthy body leads naturally to encouraging a healthy mind and thought habits.

Don't be afraid to lean on support sources. It is going to be very important, especially in the first few weeks or months following a traumatic emotional experience, to be able to lean on others for support. Perhaps, your experience with narcissist abuse has left you alienated from friends and/or family. Now is the time to reconnect with those loved ones. Don't be afraid. They are probably going to be so excited to have you back they won't even press you for details. Simply accept their support and love and lean on it when you need to. When you are ready, ask if you can discuss some of the details of your abuse as a way to process and move through them.

Educating yourself about narcissists and their tactics is going to be very important as you want to arm yourself against future abusers. If you feel you were too quick to trust in your last relationship, you may need to practice setting up barriers and waiting for people to prove to you that they are trustworthy. This may be difficult for those people who are naturally generous and giving of themselves emotionally. This can be a wonderful and amazing trait, but it is important to realize that not everyone you meet is going to have good intentions. Hopefully, you never have to meet another narcissist again. But if one should cross your path, it won't hurt to have educated yourself about how exactly to spot one and move away from that influence.

One of the most important things you can do on your path to recovery to ensure your success is to forgive yourself and let go of those feelings of guilt and shame. It won't be easy to simply dismiss these feelings, especially if you've spent months or years listening to someone tell you you're not good enough or not smart or flawed in some way. This is going to take time to move away from, but it is important to make a daily habit of verbally or internally reaffirming that you are a survivor of narcissistic abuse and that you were strong enough to pull away.

Meditation can be a very helpful tool throughout this process. Begin by sitting comfortably in a space that is quiet and free of distraction. Practice breathing slowly and taking deep breaths each time you breathe in. Focus on your body in space and feel each part of your body as you breathe. There are several guided meditations available online for you to peruse if you so desire, or you may choose to come up with your own little mantra. Whatever you decide to do, try to make some time each and every day to focus in on your affirmation. Repeat the words to yourself slowly, over and over. Tell yourself that you love yourself, that you forgive yourself, that you are enough, that you are loved, that you are strong. Simply saying these words to yourself will begin to break the toxic habit and thought cycles that once plagued your mind and triggered anxiety. Eventually, you will come to a place where those negative feelings are no longer connected to the obsessive thoughts that intruded on your mind. As you practice replacing these bad thoughts with positive ones, it will become habitual and begin to feel more natural. Meditation can be kind of strange for first-time practitioners, but I encourage you to give it a try if you are struggling to move past those negative obsessive thought cycles.

Finally, do what you can to cultivate a regular sleep schedule where you get at least 8 hours of sleep. Setting aside some time at night before bedtime for meditation may be a great way to help your brain settle down and prepare for rest. Try to go to bed at the same time every night and do something calming right before. Try not to eat and snack on junk food late at night as this will keep you up longer and may disrupt your sleep.

Know that you are strong enough to move past this horrific ordeal and that you are not alone in your experience. Re-learn to love and take care of yourself and reaffirm each day that you are worth the effort of recovery.

Steel yourself should your abuser ever re-enter your life for any reason. Enforce strict boundaries and enforce a rule of no contact whatsoever. Do not answer phone calls, texts, anything. He is not worth it, and there is nothing positive that he can offer you. You have risen above that influence.

Conclusion

Thank you for making it through to the end of *Narcissistic Abuse*. Let's hope it was informative and able to provide you with all of the tools you need to achieve your goals whatever they may be.

The next step is to share what you have learned with anyone else in your life or your family's and friends' lives who you think may benefit from the information on narcissistic abuse offered in this book. As I've said many times throughout this text, the most important weapon you have against narcissistic abusers is knowledge and learning how to spot them before they have a chance to harm you. If you or someone you love has experienced narcissistic abuse firsthand, I hope that the information and advice in this book have offered some degree of comfort and help as you move forward past this awful experience. People suffer each and every day at the hands of narcissistic abusers, and it is more important now than ever before that we all help spread the knowledge and tools available to defend ourselves from potential abusers. It is possible to escape, even if you've already fallen victim. Don't underestimate the power of the human mind to overcome even the most hurtful of emotional experiences. As you wake up each morning and take steps toward recovery each day, I hope you remember the encouragement and the tips offered in this book. Also, don't be afraid to get creative and realize new ways that are personally helpful that you may be able to share with others who may share in your unique experience. There are many different ways survivors can choose from on their paths to recovery. The key is to believe in yourself and trust in your instincts and gut feelings fueling you forward and past any and all symptoms of narcissistic abuse.

Made in the USA
Columbia, SC
21 June 2019